A
Stranger
for
Christmas

G·K
Hall
&C°

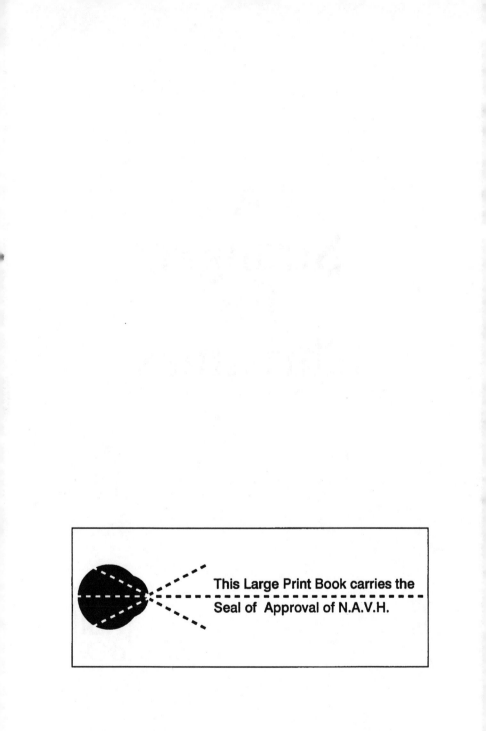

This Large Print Book carries the
Seal of Approval of N.A.V.H.

A
Stranger
for
Christmas

Carol Lynn Pearson

G.K. Hall & Co.
Thorndike, Maine

Published in 1996 by arrangement with St. Martin's Press, Inc.

G.K. Hall Large Print Inspirational Collection.

The text of this Large Print edition is unabridged.
Other aspects of the book may vary from the original edition.

Set in 18 pt. Bookman Old Style.

Printed in the United States on permanent paper.

Library of Congress Cataloging in Publication Data

Pearson, Carol Lynn.
  A stranger for Christmas / Carol Lynn Pearson.
    p.   cm.
  ISBN 0-7838-1914-5 (lg. print : hc)
  1. Large type books. I. Title.
[PS3566.E227S7 1996b]
813'.54—dc20   96-27255

A
Stranger
for
Christmas

Chapter One

"An orphan!" Florence indignantly pressed the remote control button and little orphan Annie exploded into horizontal lines and then was gone. "Now why would Daddy Warbucks go to an orphanage to get somebody to entertain for Christmas? Why didn't he go to an old folks' home and ask for a little old lady that he could entertain for Christmas?"

9

"Well," replied Myrna, brushing her long, white hair in slow, thoughtful strokes, "maybe because orphans are cuter than little old ladies. Didn't you ever notice that?"

Myrna and Florence together looked into the mirror that Florence had brought with her when she came to the convalescent home. It had a heavy gold frame and had hung in the living room of her home in Beverly Hills, situated to reflect the marble replica of Michelangelo's *David* that she had shipped home from Italy thirty years ago.

The two bodies that were reflected now in the mirror did not bear much resemblance to the *David*. They had passed their prime many years ago. Did Michelangelo do old people? If he did, he would like their faces — good, honest, wrinkled, near-transparent faces. And their hands, veined as if they were in marble already.

"Cute?" Florence leaned back in her wheelchair and closed her eyes. She used to be cute. Never beautiful. But cute — and then interesting — and then handsome. That's why she had had such a long and successful career as a character actress in Hollywood. She was never a star, but she was always useful, always in demand, right up to the time she broke her hip. And even now her red hair (red with the help of the hairdresser that came in once a month) and her strong, expressive features immediately let anyone — even the nurses — know that here was a woman of authority, a woman they could not coax into eating her squash or her green peas or her rice pudding if she didn't want to. When Florence's buzzer rang, the nurses took notice. They knew she had once played Queen Elizabeth, and they joked among themselves that she was still playing her. No one really minded, though. Florence was a bright, tough geranium in a field of wilted daisies, and the nurses all liked her, even though she made them run a lot.

"But wouldn't that be wonderful?" Florence's dramatic flair was working now. "What if tonight somebody — not Daddy Warbucks, old men don't interest me, but a family, a *family,* a real one with children and everything — walked right in the front door here and said, 'We'd like to borrow a grandma for Christmas. Let's see. That one over there, the one with the red hair, we'll take her.' "

Florence smiled and a softness crept over her Queen Elizabeth features. "And then they would take me to their home for three days, and they would hang up my stocking along with theirs by the fireplace, and we would all sing Christmas carols around the piano, and I would polish the silver for Christmas dinner, and they would ask me what Christmas

13

was like when I was a little girl, and they would tuck me in on Christmas Eve right along with the children and get me up early to open the presents, and there would be a few packages with my name on them under the tree, little things the children had made, and . . ."

Florence's voice trailed off as she was flooded by dozens of other Christmas possibilities and was suddenly too weary to choose among them. She sighed and looked over at Myrna. Then she said softly, "Wouldn't that be *wonderful?*"

Myrna smiled and finished braiding her hair into one long braid. She always liked to sleep with her hair braided; it stayed so neat. "Yes. It would be wonderful."

Florence's voice had been filled with longing. Myrna's was filled with nostalgia. Florence had never had a Christmas like that. She had never had children, never even married. Myrna had had lots of Christmases like that. The holiday season in Idaho with her husband and five children had been the kind you see pictured in *Woman's Day* and the *Ladies' Home Journal.* It had looked like, and smelled like, and tasted like, and felt like, and sounded like something close to heaven. Oh, there had been the usual tensions and even fighting between the kids. But when the Christmas season was really settled in, when all of the frantic dashing around was coming to a close, everybody seemed to soften and mellow and glow like the colored bulbs on the tree.

"Did you really make gingerbread houses?" asked Florence.

"Every year. Made a new one every year — from scratch. Made stained glass windows from candy, made a Santa Claus on his sleigh out front. January first we'd all sit down and eat the little house, Santa Claus and all. Susie couldn't stand watching us smash the house. She'd come in after it was all fallen down and take her share of the walls and dip them in milk. Mmmmmm."

Myrna had told Florence about the gingerbread house over and over. But Florence always liked to hear it again, just as Myrna's five children had always wanted to hear "The Night Before Christmas" over and over.

Myrna laid her hairbrush down on her nightstand and sighed. This year there would be no gingerbread house. This year — for the first time in all her life — there would be no family Christmas. This year there would be just her and Florence and the other old folks at the convalescent home and the nurses and the carolers that came in from the local churches.

Even after the children were all grown and married, Myrna had such good fortune that she still had them all for Christmas. They had all settled in Idaho Falls or nearby, and somehow they had worked it out agreeably for the in-laws to take Thanksgiving and New Year's and Easter and let Myrna have Christmas.

When her husband had died three years ago, just around the time Myrna's arthritis was getting severe, a family council decided that the best thing was for Myrna to go to Pasadena and live with her sister. A warmer climate, the doctor had said, would be tremendously helpful. And it had been. Myrna's fingers straightened out considerably and the pain in her knees and other joints almost went away. The children flew her home for a few weeks in the summer and then again for a short while at Christmas. And they each called once a week and sent her the little things the grandchildren were making in school.

But then her sister in Pasadena had died. And again a family council decided the best thing was for her to stay in the Southern California climate. So Richard, her eldest, had flown down and found the very best care available. Elmwood Manor was a classy place compared to most rest homes. And Richard made sure she had a telephone in her room so they could talk to her frequently. And they continued to bring her to Idaho for Christmas and in the summer.

But this Christmas — this

Christmas she would not be going. Last September she had suffered a heart attack, and her doctor felt that spending even a few days in the higher altitude would be inadvisable. So the family had decided it was best for her to stay where she was. All the children would call her on Christmas Day, and they would make a videotape of their traditional Christmas program and send it to her.

But it wouldn't be the same. Of course it wouldn't be the same. But at least she had all those years of lovely memories. Florence didn't even have the memories. It really was not fair.

"Now, why couldn't they?" demanded Florence.

"Why couldn't they what?"

"Come in here and adopt a grandma for Christmas. Why couldn't a family do that? Just once before I die I would love to have a real family Christmas — with a gingerbread house and everything."

Florence turned her wheelchair and moved herself a few feet to the window, where the cat was catching the last rays of the December sun. The manager of Elmwood Manor had read that pets were good therapy for old people, so he had brought in a cat and a dog and even put four rabbits in a hutch out in the garden. Florence had no use for the dog or the rabbits, but she readily adopted the cat, named her Kristinea after her grandmother, and would spend long hours petting her and watching her bask in the sun. Pets *were* good therapy. But people were even better. And on Christmas you needed people. A family.

Florence shook her head. "Dream on," she said, mostly to herself. "Once in a while those things happen in the movies, but only because some scriptwriter thought it'd make a good story. But not in real life. People are too busy with their own lives to bother with a stranger. Especially at Christmas. Christmas is for families. And if you don't belong — you don't belong."

"Well, no, I don't know about that, Florence," replied Myrna. "I know a lot of people, good, wonderful people, who aren't too busy to bother with a stranger."

"Oh, I'm sure you know folks that'd give canned goods to the poor or even go to the old folks' home and sing carols. But to take somebody in? To really give somebody a Christmas?" She shook her head. "Christmas started out that way — with no room for a stranger. And that's the way it'll stay. If you don't belong — you don't belong."

Myrna's eyes were troubled as she reached for her cane and made her way over to the empty chair by the window. She sat down and looked at Florence seriously. "Why, Florence, I — I don't like that."

"Well, I don't either, Myrna, but there you have it."

"I mean — well, I mean I don't *believe* it, Florence. I believe there are lots of people who have got room in their hearts — and in their home — for a stranger."

"Name one."

"Well . . . I —"

"Go on. Name one." Florence was staring at Myrna with a kind of regal defiance.

Myrna met her gaze, thought for a moment, and then spoke. "My children. Any of the five of them."

Florence laughed. She threw back her head and clapped her hands as if she had just heard a good joke. "Your children? They would sit down to dinner and say,

24

'You know what we need for Christmas? We need to find a little old lady who wants a family, and we need to bring her here for three days and let her share Christmas with us.' That's what your children would say?"

"Well, maybe not just exactly that. They might not just think it up themselves. But if it was pointed out to them — if they knew there was a little old lady who desperately needed a family for Christmas — they'd take her in, any one of them."

"A stranger?"

"A stranger."

"Strange as me?"

"Strange even as you."

"Nope. They wouldn't. Your kids are good to you. I've known some won't even send a Christmas card to their parents, but nobody — not even yours — would change their Christmas around to take in a stranger."

"Mine would."

Florence was silent a moment, then leaned in to Myrna. "Would not."

Myrna leaned in and looked unblinking into Florence's eyes. "Would too."

"Then let's find out. I say they wouldn't." Slowly Florence reached for the telephone, picked it up, and held it out to Myrna.

Chapter Two

Myrna took the telephone and looked at Florence, puzzled.

"What?" she asked.

"Call your children. Ask them if they'll take in a little old lady who needs a family for Christmas. Go on, call them."

"But — you? Take *you* in? Clear out in Idaho Falls? How could they do that?"

"No, not me. A little old lady in Idaho Falls."

Exasperated, Myrna slammed the telephone down. "But I don't *know* a little old lady in Idaho Falls who needs a family for Christmas."

Florence leaned in and spoke quietly and dramatically. "We'll make one up. We'll invent one! And if any of them says yes, they'll take her in — that'll be just about as good as if there really was one — just about as good as if they took *me* in. Why, I'd really believe in Christmas! Go ahead. Call."

Myrna hesitated. Would they say yes? She had spent long years teaching them to be good Christians, to be compassionate and caring of others. And she had set the example. She had often quoted to them that wonderful scripture:

"For I was an hungered, and ye gave me meat: I was thirsty, and ye gave me drink: I was a stranger, and ye took me in. . . . Inasmuch as ye have done it unto one of the least of these . . . ye have done it unto me."

Myrna was forever bringing home to dinner somebody who was new at church. When a funeral came up, she was the first to call and ask what she could do to help. And there was the time she took in an unwed mother and helped her through the hard times and the hard decisions. Would her children remember these things? Now that she was no longer there, would they recall the things she had tried so hard to teach them? "There's always room for one more," she would say. She would even put a few extra plates into the picnic basket in case they'd be needed. Had her children really learned the lesson she had devoted her life to teaching? Did she dare to find out? *I was a stranger, and ye took me in.*"

Slowly Myrna nodded her head and then looked at Florence. "All right. All right — I'll call them and I'll ask. But — what do I say?"

Florence's eyes lit up and she straightened her spine, pursed her lips, and leaned back to create. "Tell them about — Genevieve."

"Genevieve?"

"That's her name — Genevieve."

Myrna nodded. "Very well. I always liked that song, didn't you?" In a high, quavering voice, she began to sing, " 'Oh Genevieve, sweet Genevieve. . . .' "

Florence's deeper tones joined in the next line. " '. . . The days may come, the days may go.' Good. It's Genevieve."

"Tell me about her."

Florence opened the sliding door and Kristinea jumped onto her lap. "Well, Genevieve is eighty-five years old and she lives in a rest home in Idaho Falls, Rosemont Convalescent."

"Rosemont," Myrna repeated. "Why do they always call rest homes by the name of a flower or a tree? I think they want to trick you into thinking it's a resort of some kind. All right — Rosemont."

"And Genevieve —"

"What's her last name?"

"Christensen," Florence said, as if trying to remember. "Or is it . . ."

"Christensen's fine. I like Christensen."

With the ease of a good storyteller, Florence gestured with one hand and petted the cat with the other. "Genevieve has been confined to a wheelchair for eight years after suffering a stroke that may have been brought on by the disaster of her house burning down on the Fourth of July. They think a neighbor boy was playing with fireworks. Genevieve was desolate, of course, as all her important papers as well as thousands of dollars in antiques and of course her best dresses all went up in flames."

Myrna frowned. "It must have been awful for her."

Florence shook her head and petted Kristinea energetically. "Dreadful. Just dreadful."

"Did she have any children?"

"Three children. But none of them would take her in. Genevieve had a tragic life from the outset. Tragic. On a foolish impulse at sixteen, she married a ne'er-do-well, who also turned out to be an alcoholic. Five years and three children later, he abandoned her in a small town in Connecticut. He had sold every

35

possession except a small rocking chair brought over from England, and that, naturally, went in the fire. So, of course, Genevieve had a stroke."

"Of course."

"Genevieve came to Idaho after a second marriage to a man who inherited a potato farm there. It was also a tragic union, for he left her for the town librarian, and Genevieve was alone again at the age of fifty-two. Her three children live in the East. Only one of them even corresponds with her. Christmas after Christmas she is alone."

"Why the town librarian?"

"Well, don't ask me. That's just the way it was!"

Myrna looked questioningly at

Florence. "It *was?*"

"And now, as Christmas approaches, Genevieve's fondest wish — perhaps even her dying wish — is to spend that day with a family, to have a *real family Christmas!*" Florence's enthusiasm suddenly dissolved and her smile faded. "But she won't have it. Nobody — *nobody* will take in Genevieve for Christmas."

Resolutely Myrna picked up the telephone receiver. "Yes, they will. Richard — my eldest son Richard — he'll take her in for Christmas." She reached out to dial, then hesitated.

"Go on — go on."

"I . . . I've never lied to my children. I don't lie to anybody.

There really isn't a Genevieve, you know."

"Isn't there? Isn't Genevieve anybody who needs a Christmas and won't get one? There must be thousands of Genevieves. Go on."

Myrna breathed deeply and reached again to dial. She had to do it now. She had to do it for Florence, who needed to know there was someone who would take her in. But more than that, she had to do it for herself. She needed to know that her children had learned what she had spent so many years trying to teach them. Had they learned? Would they say yes?

Myrna's hand shook as she reached in the drawer for her little address book. She used to have all the children's numbers memorized, but her mind wasn't quite as trustworthy as it used to be.

"Here it is. Richard. Have I told you about Richard?"

"Three times a week."

"Richard is my oldest, and, you know, there's something very special about the relationship of a mother to her oldest child. Three times we dreamed the very same dream on the same night. I always knew what he was feeling, and he always seemed to know what I was feeling. In fact, when I had my heart attack, he called the very next hour to see what was the matter. He's a high school principal. Has four children of his own."

"Four? And into that crowd he'll bring another, a stranger?"

"If I ask him to." Myrna nodded her head firmly. "I think Richard would do anything in the world that I asked him to do."

Florence picked up the receiver and held it out to Myrna. Myrna took a deep breath, pressed her hands together as if in prayer, and then reached for the telephone.

Chapter Three

"Hello?"

"Hi, darlin'. It's Grandma."

"Oh, hi, Grandma. How are you?"

"Fine. Fine."

"Is it snowing there, Grandma?"

"Snow? Of course not."

"Well, Robby said that once about ten years ago it snowed in Los Angeles, and I thought maybe it would do it again. Then you could at least have a white

43

Christmas. I sure wish you were coming this year, Grandma."

"Yes. Me too. Well — is your daddy there?"

"He's out in the garage building something. He told me not to come out, but I'll just knock on the door and tell him you want him. Hang on. Love you, Grandma."

"Love you too, darlin'." Myrna put a hand over the receiver and whispered loudly to Florence. "That's Julie, such a sweetheart — you should hear her play the piano."

Florence nodded but did not reply. Her eyes were fixed un-blinkingly on Myrna and her hands clasped and unclasped nervously. She moistened her lips and leaned forward a little.

"Mother?"

Myrna jumped. "Hello. Rich-ard?"

"How are you? Everything okay?"

"Yes. Fine. Fine. And you?"

"Just great. Santa Claus is staying up until one to get some things done, but other than miss-ing a little sleep *and* trying to keep the snowball fights under control at the high school, every-thing's fine. But it's cold here — reminds me of that time we were snowed in at school for four days. Remember?"

"I remember." Myrna almost laughed. "You thought that was as much fun as Disneyland." She paused, then hurried on, pushing the words out before she lost courage. 'Uh — Richard — sweetheart — there's something I want to ask you — something I want to ask you to do."

"Sure, Mother. What is it?"

"Well, there's a woman in a rest home right there in Idaho Falls — Rosemont Convalescent. She's sort of a friend of mine. I mean, I haven't actually met her, but — uh, hang on." Quickly Myrna covered the receiver and turned to Florence. *"How do I know Genevieve?"* she whispered loudly.

"You've been writing," Florence whispered back. "You're pen pals. It's a program of the rest homes. Three years ago —"

Myrna held up her hand to silence her.

"Richard? We've been corresponding, Genevieve and I. That's her name — Genevieve Christensen. And we've gotten to be very close. Genevieve has had a tragic life. Just tragic. And more than anything else in the whole world Genevieve would like, before she dies, to have a real family Christmas. You know, the kind we've always had. I was wondering — well, what I'm asking, Richard, is that you and your family take her in for three days and give her a *real* Christmas."

Myrna paused. "Richard?"

"You mean — here? Bring her here to our home?"

"That's it exactly. Right into

your home. She gets around quite well with the aid of her wheelchair. I really don't think she'd be much trouble."

There was a long pause, and then Richard spoke. "What about her family? Wouldn't they —"

"Oh, no. Genevieve has no family. No real family. There are three children in the East, but they're of absolutely no value to her. No value at all. In actual fact, she has no one."

There was an embarrassed silence, and then Richard spoke. "Uh, Mother — could you hang on for just a minute? I need to speak to Rosemary."

Myrna covered the receiver again and once more whispered to Florence. "He's talking to Rosemary. Lovely girl. A wonderful mother."

A full minute passed before Richard came back to the telephone.

"Uh — Mother?"

"Yes?"

"The problem is this. Becky's bringing home her fiancé from college. We haven't even met him yet. So that means putting the two younger ones together to make a place for him. I'm afraid — there just wouldn't be room."

"What about the hide-a-bed?"

Another silence. "Mother, this is sort of a special time for Becky. I'm afraid that — well, having a stranger here and all . . . would sort of . . . you know . . ." Helplessly his voice trailed off.

"Yes. I know."

"But we'll be glad to take a plate of cookies over to her," Richard hurriedly continued. "Was that — Rosemont?"

"No, don't bother. She — she can't have sugar."

"I'm sorry, Mother. But you understand."

"I understand."

"We'll call you on Christmas. I love you, Mother."

"Love you too, Richard. Goodbye."

Slowly Myrna put the receiver back on the telephone.

Florence rocked back and forth, holding Kristinea tight against her chest. "He said no."

Myrna raised her head and looked at Florence silently for a

moment, then spoke rapidly. "But he had a good reason. A very good reason. Their oldest daughter is bringing her fiancé home for Christmas, and it just wouldn't be . . . comfortable. Genevieve wouldn't want to make Becky uncomfortable."

"No." Florence's face looked older than it had five minutes ago. "Only — it's always uncomfortable. It's always inconvenient. I'm inconvenient. Genevieve's inconvenient. We don't belong."

"Now, that's not so, Florence. Richard had an unusual circumstance. One of my children — at least *one* of them — will take Genevieve in."

Florence sighed and settled back. "Who's next?"

"Beverly. Have I told you about Beverly?"

Florence nodded. "You've told me about Beverly."

The door swished open and Ruth entered with two dinner trays. Ruth was always bright and cheerful, even when those she attended were cranky. "Dinnertime!" she sang out. "Chicken Surprise!"

"That's no surprise," observed Florence, nudging Kristinea out of her lap and wheeling herself to the sink to wash her hands.

". . . 'Tis the season to be jolly. . . ." Ruth sang on. She was one of those rare people who seem always to enjoy whatever thing they happen to be doing at any given moment. She was about forty, with a good, slim figure and a face that wore just a bit too much color on the cheeks and just a bit too long eyelashes on her eyes. But the eyelashes were the only thing about her that was false. Her good cheer and deep caring for the patients at Elmwood had made her a favorite of them all.

"Ruth?" Florence's tones had become regal again. "Are those canned peas? Canned peas are disgusting — lifeless, offensive little creatures. I told the kitchen I never wanted to see another one again as long as I lived."

Ruth picked up one of the offensive little creatures between her thumb and forefinger and squashed it. "You're right. Canned peas are disgusting. I will remind the kitchen that canned peas are never to darken your door again."

The offenders were quickly scooped into a napkin and disposed of in the wastebasket.

"Is this less disgusting?" With exaggerated secrecy Ruth pulled from her pocket a Hershey candy bar and laid it ceremoniously on Florence's tray.

"Ah!" With a cry of delight, Florence entered into the drama, reverently picked up the candy bar, and pressed it to her bosom.

"Don't you dare tell, now. The doctor said chocolate is off limits for you. But I've seen all those candy wrappers in your wastebasket. I don't know who's pushing it, but I know you're getting the stuff from somewhere. But for the last two weeks — no candy wrappers. I figured you must be getting desperate, so I picked some up on the way to work this morning."

She pulled a second candy bar from her pocket. "I even got one for Myrna, although I don't think she's a chocoholic like *other* people we could mention."

"Why, thanks, Ruth." Myrna smiled as she accepted the Hershey bar. "Only rarely do I indulge. Tonight I will indulge."

"*After* the Chicken Surprise and salad and bread and milk. Promise?"

"Promise."

Ruth squeezed two shoulders and swept out of the room. "I'll check on you in twenty minutes."

The two women sat in silence as they cut up their Chicken Surprise. Then Myrna gestured toward the door with her knife and said, "Now, there's a lovely human being. You see, Florence? The world is full of lovely human beings who would go out of their way for you."

Florence nodded. "Ruth's a lovely person. She'll go into a grocery store to get you a chocolate bar. That takes ten minutes. And she'll stay late to listen to you finish a story. Five minutes. All I'm saying is that there are limits to what anybody'll do for anybody else. And Genevieve is pushing against the limits. To rearrange three days of your life for a stranger — that's more than a candy bar. That's more than anybody'd do."

"You're wrong, Florence. And as soon as I finish this Chicken Surprise and this salad and this bread and milk and this Hershey bar, Beverly and I are going to show you just how wrong you are."

Chapter Four

Florence nervously broke off small bits of her Hershey bar and ate them while Myrna opened her blue-flowered address book.

"Let's see." Myrna reached for her glasses and then adjusted them on her nose as she held the address book up to the light of the lamp. "Ah, here it is. Beverly and Tom. We had a hard time getting Beverly here. Did I tell you

61

that? She almost didn't make it. The doctors, in fact, told me she was a miracle baby. For two weeks they didn't expect her to live. But she surprised them all."

A gentle smile crept over Myrna's face and she laid the address book down in her lap. "When I took her home from the hospital we had to carry her around on a pillow, she was that skinny. But when she decided to grow, she really grew. By her first birthday her little knees were so chubby. And dimples? My land — dimples!" Myrna stared at the curtains, caught in the folds of a time warp.

"Myrna!" said Florence impatiently. "Just make the call!"

But Myrna was not listening.

"That first Christmas we hung up one of her teeny tiny baby stockings. Just that big! And Richard and I sang to her over and over —

"Hang up
   the baby's stocking,
And don't you
   dare forget.
For the dear little
   dimpled darling
Has never seen
   Christmas yet.
I've told her all about it,
And she opened her
   big blue eyes.
I'm sure she
   understood me —
For she looked
   so very wise."

Myrna nodded her head in satisfaction. "Yes, I think Beverly's is the right home for Genevieve. I really do. And she has more than enough room. Her husband's a dentist — did three root canals for me a few years ago. So they have enough money. And the household is very organized — runs like a well-oiled machine. Both children are in high school — *terribly* active in *everything* — a boy and a girl. Beverly does a lot of volunteer work for community services."

"Myrna! Just make the call!"

"Yes, I think Beverly is the right home for Genevieve."

Myrna picked up the telephone receiver, squinted at the address book, and pushed the buttons.

She took a few deep breaths and closed her eyes as she listened to the ringing on the other end.

"Hello?" The voice sounded far away and wrapped in static.

"Beverly?"

"Hello? Mother?"

"I can't hear you very well, Beverly."

"What? I can't hear you, Mother. I've got my mixer going. Just a minute; I'll turn it off."

Myrna covered the receiver with her hand and spoke to Florence. "She had her mixer going. She's turning it off."

"Mother?"

"Now I can hear you. How are you, Beverly?"

"Fine. And you?"

"Fine."

"What are you up to, Mother? Keeping out of mischief?"

Myrna smiled. Beverly always asked her that. As if there were a great deal of mischief she could get into at Elmwood.

"Oh, yes. I'm behaving myself well. You'd be proud of me. What are you mixing?"

"Danish Christmas Cookies. That great recipe of yours. Remember?"

"Remember! I must have made ten thousand Danish Christmas Cookies in my day. How are the kids?"

"Just great. Shall I put them on?"

"No. It's you I want to talk to. Beverly . . ."

"Yes?"

"I want to ask a favor of you. It's sort of a big one, but it's important to me." Myrna paused and pressed her fingers to her forehead.

"What is it, Mother?"

"It's Genevieve. I'm terribly concerned about her."

"Genevieve?"

"She's at Rosemont Convalescent, there in Idaho Falls. We've been corresponding for some time and she's just one of the loveliest people you'd ever want to meet. But she's terribly lonely. Oh, Beverly, she is *so* lonely. I think about Genevieve and it just breaks my heart. One husband left her for alcohol and the other left her for the town librarian. Three children in the East that she *never* sees."

"Why does she live in Idaho?"

"That's where the potato farm was. Anyway — Genevieve wants, just once before she dies, to spend a real Christmas with a real family — with stockings by the fire, and a tree, and Danish Christmas Cookies. She loves cookies!"

"Mother?" Beverly's voice had taken on an apprehensive tone. "You mean — you mean you want us to bring her from the rest home here, to our house, and have her as a guest for Christmas?"

"Three days. Just three days. You'd love her, Beverly. The kids and Tom would love her. She's had a tragic life, but she is so bright and cheerful."

"Here?"

"She does require a wheelchair, but she can get in and out of bed by herself."

There was a long pause.

"Beverly? Are you there?"

"What? Oh, yes. I'm just . . . just trying to think this through."

"I think, of all the children, you're the right choice, Beverly. I know you'll give Genevieve a Christmas she'll never forget."

"Uh — Mother. I don't know how to — Mother, listen. We can't. We just can't."

"Well, why not?"

Beverly was obviously caught off guard. Myrna knew when her children were fishing for an excuse. Years ago Beverly had told her she didn't want to take piano lessons anymore because the piano keys were too hard and they hurt her fingers.

"Beverly?" Myrna tried to speak the name with the right amount of authority and humility.

"Mother, it's like this. We're hardly even going to be home at all. We've got so many things planned, we're just going to be running, running the whole time. The kids have this and that they've got to be to — and Tom and I —"

"Well, take her with you."

"In a wheelchair? In and out on these icy streets? I'd be terrified that she'd hurt herself."

"Then leave her home."

"Alone? That would be awful. I

couldn't leave her here by herself. She'd feel terribly neglected. Mother — I just don't see how we could possibly work it out. I'm — I'm sorry. But I'll certainly make sure that the chorus from the kids' high school puts her rest home on its list for caroling. Rosemont, was it?"

"Yes." Myrna's voice was quiet and empty.

"And her name was —"

"Genevieve."

Beverly's voice suddenly brightened, as a mother's does when she's trying to distract a disappointed child. "We'll call you on Christmas, Mother. Sleep tight. Love you."

"I love you too, Beverly. Good night."

Myrna sat staring at the telephone receiver for a full minute
before she reached over and hung
it up. Beverly had remembered
the recipe for the Danish Christmas Cookies, but she hadn't remembered what Christmas was
really about. It wasn't about
cookies. It wasn't at all about
cookies. *I was a stranger, and ye
took me in.*

Florence spoke softly. "Don't
call the rest, Myrna. Don't call
them."

Myrna considered. "I've got to
know. I *have to know.* It's not
possible that all of them — is it?"

"Then call them in the morning."

Myrna shook her head. "I
couldn't sleep. I've got to call to-

night." She picked up the address book, then hesitated and looked over at Florence, confused.

"Florence? How old is Genevieve — exactly?"

Florence thought a moment, then replied. "Eighty-five."

"She won't have many more years, will she?"

"No, she won't."

Resolutely, Myrna picked up her address book. "Joy," she said. "Have I told you about Joy?"

Chapter
Five

"Bedtime!" Ruth entered the room, efficiently picking up two well-cleaned trays. "Good girls!" She placed the trays on the rolling rack in the hallway and then returned. "Come on, Florence. You first. Let's get your 'jammies' on."

"So soon? It isn't even eight yet," said Myrna in the voice of a child who wants to watch just one more television show.

"Now, now!" chimed Ruth. " 'Better not pout, better not cry, better watch out, I'm tellin' you why —' " She frowned. "Or is it 'Better watch out, better not cry —' It's been too long since my kids were little."

"Ruth — we need a few more minutes. We've got to make some phone calls — some very important phone calls. Just give us another half hour. Please?"

"Ah, secrets, huh? Gettin' a hot date for New Year's Eve? You're not allowed to stay out until midnight, you know, dancing and cavorting around like shameless hussies."

Her brightness was infectious. Even Myrna smiled. "The only hot date I'm planning for New Year's is with a cup of hot milk."

"Wise woman. A cup of milk is something you can count on. But a man? He's never there when you need him. Take it from me, okay? Just because it's Christmas, I'll do everybody else first and you can be last. And remember, if I catch you sneaking out of here on New Year's Eve to meet some men from the rest home up the street at the corner drugstore — you are gonna be in *big trouble!*"

Ruth paused to wipe a few crumbs from Florence's front and then left.

Now, why would she say that, Myrna wondered — that business about a man never being there when you need him. Her Sidney had always been loyal. Evidently

Ruth had had some bad experiences. And both of Genevieve's husbands had left her. Was it true that you just can't count on most people? But not — certainly not your own children. Certainly a woman can count on her own children. Well, Genevieve couldn't. They were all three back East and only one of them ever even sent her a card. But her own children were different. She had always been able to count on them. Always. Myrna reached out again for the address book and opened it.

"Did I tell you why we named her Joy?"

"Why?"

"Because that's what she was. Such a joy. I know the books say

80

that babies can't smile for the first few weeks, that it's only gas. But I tell you Joy smiled. The minute we got home from the hospital, she smiled. Did I ever tell you about Joy's goldfish?"

"Goldfish? No."

Myrna chuckled. "Well, Joy won this goldfish at the carnival at school. And she put it in a bowl right there on the kitchen counter. And every morning as she was eating breakfast she would watch that little fish and talk to it. Of course, she was supposed to keep the bowl clean, but sometimes she didn't do a very good job of it. Well, one morning, when she had neglected her duties for some time and the goldfish bowl was *quite* disgusting, somehow she talked me into just changing the water for her and she would do a real cleaning when she got back from school."

Florence nodded. "Ah, yes."

"Now, I had never owned a goldfish and so I had never changed the water for one. I took it over to the sink, fished the little creature out with a small sieve, and watched as it flipped itself out and slid into the sink and down the drain. Right down the drain. Right before my eyes!"

Florence began to laugh, and Myrna laughed with her.

"What was I to do? It was gone forever! Well, I hurried out to the car and I drove down to the local pet shop. And I walked in and I said to the clerk, 'Please show me to your goldfish. I have just dropped my daughter's goldfish down the kitchen sink, and I need to get another one before she comes home from school.' "

"And what did the clerk say to that?"

"He said, 'Lady, it won't work. A child knows her own goldfish.' I said, 'Just show me to the goldfish.' So we went back to where the goldfish were. And they were all exactly one-half the size of the fish I had dropped down the drain."

Florence clapped her hands together and laughed out loud.

"So I bought two."

The story came to a halt while both women gave in to laughter, rocking back and forth like wind-up dolls.

"When I got home," Myrna continued when she had caught her breath, "when I got home, I put the two little goldfish in the bowl and didn't say a word about it. Well, Joy did not clean the bowl that evening, and the next morning as we were having breakfast, she suddenly said, 'There's two goldfish in that bowl!' And Richard said, 'Don't be dumb, there's not two goldfish in that bowl.' Well, Joy stood up and pointed and said, 'Yes, there is! Look! There's two goldfish in that bowl!' So they all looked — and sure enough, there were two goldfish in the bowl. And then *I* said, 'Joy, I cannot tell a lie. I did it. I dropped your goldfish, and I broke it. I broke it *right in two!* "

Florence laughed again, laughed until tears rolled down her cheeks.

"Well, they all stared at me in amazement, and they laughed, and I laughed, and I told them what had happened, and *that's* the story of the goldfish."

It felt good to laugh. Myrna had not laughed for quite a while, and it felt good. Her home had always been filled with laughter. And caring. And going out of her way to do things with the children and for them. She had not *had* to rush down to the pet store to replace the goldfish. She had not *had* to do any of the other hundreds of things, thousands of things, she had done for her children above and beyond the call of duty. She had done them because she wanted to, because she loved to. Everything her children had asked of her — everything that she felt was good and right — she went out of her way to do. Surely — surely they would do the same for her. Maybe this was just a really bad time for Richard and Beverly. That was it — the timing. But Joy would not let her down. Joy would say, "Of course, Mother. What's the address?" Cheered and renewed from the good laugh, Myrna picked up the telephone receiver and dialed. She counted the rings. Five — six — seven — eight. Myrna was about to hang up. Then —

"Hello?" It was a man's voice.

"Hello? Is this Paul?"

"Mother? How are you?"

"Fine."

"We were just running out to go to a program over at the church. Let me get Joy."

"Thanks, Paul." Myrna covered the receiver and whispered loudly to Florence. "He's going to get Joy. They were just on their way out."

"Hello? Are you all right, Mother?"

"Yes. Yes, I'm fine."

"Are you sure?" Joy could always tell if Myrna tried to hide anything.

"I'm *fine*. Only —"

"Only what, Mother? You haven't had another heart attack, have you? Mother?"

"No. No. Joy, I . . . I need something. I need you to do me a favor."

"Yes?"

"Not for me, really. For somebody else. For Genevieve. She's a friend of mine who lives in a rest home not far from you in Idaho Falls. She's eighty-five years old and she won't have many more Christmases and she's had a very sad life, and she wants very much — *very much* — to spend just one Christmas with a real family. Both her husbands left her, and her three children back East couldn't care less whether she lives or dies. Genevieve is a lovely person, and I want — I want to give her a present this Christmas.

I want to give her Christmas. I want her to spend it — with you."

There was silence on the other end of the telephone. That same long silence.

"Here? You want Genevieve to come and spend Christmas here with us?"

"That's what I'm asking, Joy. I'm asking it as a favor to Genevieve, but mostly as a favor to me. I'm asking you to take Genevieve in for three days and give her a wonderful, wonderful Christmas."

Another pause.

"Mother? Can you hang on for a moment? I really ought to discuss this with Paul."

"Certainly. Go talk it over with Paul."

Myrna put her hand over the receiver and turned to Florence, but Florence spoke first. "I know. She's talking it over with Paul."

Myrna heard just a hint of a hushed conversation, and then Joy was back on the line.

"Mother . . . if . . . if it were any other time — but — Gina has got a cold — a bad, a very bad cold. And it might even be more than that. The doctor wants to run tests for strep throat and he was even talking about mononucleosis. Anyway, it would be a terrible thing to bring in an old person and expose her to something. Old people are so fragile. I would just feel terrible if she caught something here. You can see that, can't you, Mother?"

"Yes." Myrna spoke quietly. "I can see that. Well, Joy — Merry Christmas."

"We'll call you on Christmas Day, Mother. I've got to run now or we'll be late for the program."

"Yes. You run. Good-bye, Joy."

"Good-bye, Mother."

Myrna lowered the receiver into her lap and noticed it again only when the dial tone turned into a growing buzz. Then she hung it up and looked over at Florence, who was petting Kristinea wordlessly.

After a moment Florence spoke. "Let's go to bed, Myrna."

"Well," Myrna said slowly. "Maybe she's right. Maybe it would not be fair to take Genevieve in if there's sickness.

We wouldn't want Genevieve to get sick, would we?"

Florence did not reply.

"Did I tell you about Dale?" Without waiting for an answer, Myrna reached again for her address book.

Chapter Six

"Hello?"

"Hello. It's Grandma. Who am I speaking to?"

"Bradley. Hi, Grandma."

"Is your daddy there, Bradley?"

"No. They just went to the store. They're supposed to be back by now. Should I tell him something?"

"Yes. Would you please tell him to call me, Bradley? Tell him it's very important and he should call me right away. Can you do that?"

"Sure."

"You won't forget?"

"I'll tell him. 'Bye, Grandma."

"Bye, Bradley."

Myrna hung up the telephone and looked at Florence. "Now that I think about it, Dale is really the best choice for someone to take in Genevieve. Dale works for the welfare department. He's very sensitive to people's needs. Last year he told me about a family he was working with. The father had been unemployed for six months and a little girl needed an expensive operation. Dale got the Lions Club and the Kiwanis Club and I don't know who else together and they raised the money. It was just wonderful."

"It was his job."

"Why, no, it wasn't."

"He got paid for it. It isn't hard to be nice to people when you get paid for it. Ruth gets paid for it too."

"Why — but —" Myrna tried to think of a good answer for that. Dale did get paid for working with that family. But he didn't have to work for them so hard as he had. And Ruth did get paid for what she did for Florence and Myrna. But she could still be paid and not be quite so nice.

"Would your son have raised the money for that operation if it had not been for his job?"

Myrna considered. There was no way she could know that. And if Ruth lost her job here, would they ever see her again? There was no way she could know that, either. But as soon as the phone rang, she would know — she would know if —

"All right, ladies, bedtime!" Ruth entered and headed straight for the chest of drawers and took out two nightgowns.

"Not yet, Ruth. Please, he'll be calling in just a few minutes. Please."

"Aha! Caught you. You *are* planning some big rendezvous for New Year's Eve. I've got to keep my eye on you, you sly one."

Myrna responded with a weak smile. "It's my son. And it's terribly important. Just ten more minutes. Please."

Something in her voice made

Ruth kneel down and look into her eyes. Then she looked over at Florence, whose eyes were on the cat in her lap.

"Are you all right? Hey, is something wrong? Can I help?"

"No," Myrna lied. "Nothing's wrong. I just . . . I just have to speak to my son."

"Sure, Myrna. Sure. I'll be back later."

Ruth stood up and was about to leave when Myrna caught her by the hand.

"Ruth?"

"Yes?"

"If you didn't work here anymore — if you were transferred or found another job — we'd never see you again, would we?"

Ruth knelt down again and

reached over to touch Myrna's cheek. "Never see me again? Why, you couldn't get rid of me that easy, Myrna. I'd come see you all the time — and make sure you were eating your veggies — and sneak in a candy bar or two. Sure you'd see me again. What are you talking about?"

Myrna smiled. "Promise?"

Ruth held up three fingers of her right hand. "On my honor as a Girl Scout — which I never was but I don't lie anyway — I promise that I would come see you a lot even if I got fired, which I might do if I don't get you ladies to bed pretty soon. Okay?"

Nodding, Myrna let go of Ruth's hand. "Okay."

When they were alone again,

Myrna positioned the telephone about a foot in front of her and folded her hands in her lap. Florence wheeled herself around to face Myrna and sat petting the purring Kristinea. Both women stared at the telephone.

Ring, ring! Myrna thought, concentrating all her energies on the red little instrument. Richard had asked her what color telephone she wanted and she chose red. Black was too businesslike. White was too hospitalish. Red seemed friendly. Maybe red would ring more. *Ring, ring!* she thought again. She used to talk to her arthritis when it got really bad, and sometimes it had seemed to help.

The telephone rang and both

women jumped.

"Hello?"

"Mother? Are you all right?"

"I'm fine. How are you, Dale?"

"Okay. But I was worried. Bradley said it was important. Is there something wrong?"

"Oh, no. No. Not with *me*. I mean, there is something — wrong. It's Genevieve."

"Who?"

And here it came again — the story of Genevieve, her tragic life, her deep desire to have a real Christmas with a real family just once before she died.

"Here? You want me to bring her here for Christmas?"

"Would you, Dale? It would mean so much to me."

"You're serious? A woman you

haven't even met?"

"Why, yes. Just do for her what you would do for me. I won't be there, you know. Just let her — take my place."

Again there was the uncomfortable silence. Myrna made tiny pleats of her skirt, pressing them into her lap.

"Well, Mother . . . you see . . . I really feel bad about this, but it just wouldn't be possible. Marta has had a really terrible time these last couple of months."

"Oh? You didn't tell me about that."

"Well, I . . ." Dale paused vaguely and then hurried on. "She's been having headaches, and things at her job are not going well. Putting this kind of a strain on her — I don't know. Christmas is a real challenge just by itself. I couldn't ask her to bring in a total stranger at that time. With everything else she has to do I couldn't ask her to wait on an invalid."

"Oh, Genevieve's not an invalid. She — she walks a mile every day."

Florence stopped petting the cat and looked up, surprised. "She does?"

Myrna put her hand over the receiver and whispered loudly to Florence. "I think it's the wheel-chair. I think the wheelchair frightens them." Then she spoke back into the telephone. "Dale? Genevieve is a very hardy person. In fact, I think if you wanted to

go ice skating, you could prob-
ably just take her along."

"At eighty-five? You're kid-
ding."

"And she'd be great to help the
kids build a snowman."

Florence rolled her eyes and
went back to petting the cat.

"Well, Mother, you know I'd love
to do anything for you. Anything
I could. This is just something
that — that I can't." He paused.
"Mother? Are you there?"

"Well, thanks anyway, Dale.
Nice to talk to you."

"I'll call you on Christmas,
Mother. What would be the best
time to —"

Myrna's shaking hand hung up
the telephone. It remained grasp-
ing the red receiver while a small

wet drop fell onto the white skin and ran in a little rivulet between the veins. Was this really happening? Dale had said no? Dale, whom she had sat up with seven nights running when he had pneumonia? Dale too had said no?

"Bedtime!" There was that cheerful voice again. There was Ruth breezing in as bright as a sleigh bell.

"Yes," said Myrna softly. "Yes, it's bedtime."

Chapter
Seven

Lying in bed that night, Myrna and Florence watched the end of a Christmas special on television. All the old-time Christmas sights and sounds and feelings flooded them and wrapped around them like a blanket. But not a warm blanket. It felt cold somehow.

Soon the lights were turned out and the only sound was the breathing of the two women and the clink of dishes somewhere down the hall.

"Florence?"

"Hmmm?"

"Are you asleep?"

"No. Are you?"

"Do you want to play 'I'm thinking of a person'?"

Sometimes, when neither one could sleep, they passed the time by playing their favorite game. One would think of a person and the other would have to guess who it was by asking questions that could be answered yes or no. Some of their favorites had been Joan of Arc, Napoleon, Eleanor Roosevelt, and Elizabeth Taylor. Florence had been stuck for a full hour once on Betsy Ross.

"All right," said Florence. "I'm

thinking of a person.

"Genevieve," said Myrna quickly.

"How did you know?" asked Florence.

Myrna did not reply to the question, but asked another. "What do you suppose Genevieve's thinking right now?"

Florence considered. "Alone. Alone again. Alone again at Christmas."

Myrna clicked her tongue and shook her head in the dark. "Poor Genevieve. Alone again." If you had pushed her, Myrna would have admitted that in actual fact Genevieve was not a real person. But in another way, a very real kind of way, Genevieve was as real as *she* was.

The two women were silent for a few moments, and then Florence spoke. "Your turn. Go ahead."

"All right. Let's see. I'm thinking of a person."

"Alive?"

"Yes."

"Female?"

"Yes."

"Famous?"

"No."

"Have I met her?"

"No."

Florence paused. "Have I ever *heard* of her?"

"Mmmmm. Maybe."

"*Maybe?* This isn't your second-grade schoolteacher again, is it?" A few months ago that one had made Florence so mad she wouldn't play the game for two weeks.

"No. No. Oh, I'm not in the mood for this game, Florence. Susie. I was thinking of Susie."

"Susie?"

"My youngest daughter, Susie. Did I ever tell you about Susie?"

"A little."

Myrna didn't need any encouragement. Stories about Susie came flooding out: how Susie had such a tender heart that she brought home every stray cat in town and begged to keep it; how she found a little garter snake that had had its tail cut off and talked Myrna into letting her keep it in a box in her room and try to heal it; how she cried even during sad television commercials.

"Now that I think about it, Susie is really the best candidate for taking Genevieve in. Last fall she helped her twins nurse back to health a little bird they found on their way home from school. Now, if she would take in a little bird, don't you think she would take in Genevieve?"

"Maybe so," said Florence, without meaning it.

"Did I tell you about the twins?" Without waiting for a reply, she went on. "They just turned ten — darling little girls, blond hair in the longest ponytails you've ever seen, on either side of their heads. It's the twins that start out the Christmas program — ever since they were four. They come out looking just like little angels with long white robes and tinsel halos and they say together — 'Christmas is a time of love, a time of peace, a time to remember Christ. Listen to the Christmas story.' "

Myrna's voice broke a little as she said those last words. She would not be there this year to hear the twins introduce the program. And the worst thought of all — why have the program anyway? "A time to remember Christ." Were they remembering? *"I was a stranger, and ye took me in."*

But there was one hope left. Susie. First thing in the morning, even before Ruth came in with their breakfast trays, Myrna would call Susie. Her baby — always her sweet baby — Susie would not say no. Susie would take in Genevieve. Holding this thought close to her like a comforting rag doll, Myrna slept.

Even the cat was still asleep the next morning when Myrna reached for her address book.

"So early?" asked Florence, opening one eye to look at the clock. "It's only six-thirty."

"It's later in Idaho than it is here," replied Myrna. "Besides, Susie has always been an early riser."

Myrna pulled her robe tighter around her and repeated the little prayer that had been playing over and over in her mind all night as if on a record. "Please — please let Susie say yes. Please, let her say yes."

She dialed the number and then closed her eyes.

"Hello?"

"Hello. It's Grandma."

"Hi, Grandma."

"Now, I know I've got one of the twins, but which one do I have?"

"Sara."

"Well, Sara. How are you, my dear?"

"Fine, Grandma. How are you?"

"Very well, thank you. Is your mother there?"

"I'll get her."

Myrna pulled out from under the bed the good warm slippers the twins had given her last Christmas. It was chilly first thing in the morning here and she always appreciated the slippers.

"Mother? How are you?"

"Fine, Susie. And you?"

"Oh, Mother, you should see our tree this year. It's never been so beautiful. Aunt Mabel made me three dozen of those little tatted snowflakes. And I got some more —"

"Susie?" Myrna could wait no longer. "Susie — I — I need your help."

"What is it?" Susie's voice was alarmed.

"I need you to — to take in a friend of mine for Christmas."

And here it came for the fifth time, the tale of Genevieve, her disappointments, her sorrows, her loneliness, her hope of having one family Christmas — just *one family Christmas* — before she died. Myrna told it better this time than she had ever told it before. And her voice was close to breaking.

"Just let her be the grandma this year, Susie. Let her take my place. Give her a Christmas that will let her die happy."

Myrna waited for a response. There was none.

"Susie?"

"Mother — this is — well, I need to think about this for a minute. Can I call you back?"

"No, Susie. Just tell me now, yes or no."

Again there was no response.

"She'd be hardly any trouble at all. She doesn't have a wheelchair or anything. She walks a mile a day, in fact."

"But . . . but wouldn't she be awfully uncomfortable — with strangers?"

"She'd love it. Believe me, she'd love it."

"But we're — I mean, it just isn't a good time. The timing's all wrong, Mother. Maybe I could do it next year. I'm quite sure I could next year. I'd plan for it."

"She won't be with us next year."

"She won't?"

"No. She's . . . she's fading fast."

"I thought you said she walks a mile a day."

Myrna paused. "Slowly. Slower and slower. Next year she'll be only a memory."

"Oh, Mother! I wish I could. Believe me, I wish I could. But I can't. I just can't. Please try to understand. Mother?"

"Well," said Myrna slowly. "Have a happy Christmas."

"I'll talk to you soon, Mother. And we're making that videotape of the program. I know you'll love it."

"Yes. Good-bye, Susie."

"Good-bye. Love you, Mother."

Myrna hung up the telephone and slumped back in her chair.

Florence was the first to speak. "Don't blame your kids too much, Myrna. They're good people. Now that I think about it, I wouldn't have wanted to take in a little old lady for Christmas when I was young. It only seems like a good idea to me now because I *am* a little old lady."

Myrna nodded. "I suppose so, Florence. Yes, I suppose so. I just thought that maybe mine were different." Slowly she closed her blue-flowered address book and put it back in the drawer.

Chapter Eight

The next day was the day before Christmas Eve. Caroling groups had already come twice from the local churches. Christmas music was playing almost constantly in the hallway. And cookies shaped like bells and Santas appeared on the lunch and dinner trays. Ruth was taking four days off, and she had come in the day before to wish Myrna and

Florence Merry Christmas.

"Now, you be good, and be sure to tell me what Santa Claus brings you." Ruth gave them each a kiss on the cheek as she left.

Santa Claus. Well, there would be presents to unwrap. A large box had arrived from Idaho Falls carrying a dozen or so brightly wrapped presents that were now on the table by the poinsettia, waiting for Christmas morning. Florence had a couple of presents waiting too, sent over by a cousin and by the woman who used to be her agent.

"We're not so bad off, you know, Myrna," said Florence. "There's lots who are worse off than we are."

Myrna nodded. She didn't say

it, she just thought it. Genevieve. Genevieve would have not one present at all to open. They had agreed not to mention her again. It was just too painful. Myrna tried not to think about her either, but it didn't work. That was just about all she did think about. And her children. And she listed all the good qualities of each precious child and told herself over and over that their excuses were valid. The timing was wrong. It had just been too much to ask. But that phrase kept repeating over and over in her mind like the tunes in the hallway. *"I was a stranger, and ye took me in."*

After lunch Myrna and Florence sat dozing in their chairs. They had given up taking afternoon naps; they slept better at night that way. But dozing in their chairs after lunch was a ritual they both enjoyed.

As Myrna drifted in and out of consciousness, the sounds of the rest home played through her mind — ". . . 'It came upon a midnight clear, that glorious song of old' " . . . and the clink of dishes and trays . . . and the squeak of rubber-soled shoes on the tile floor . . . and the voice of an old woman down the hall calling for a nurse . . .

And another sound — two young voices speaking together. "Christmas is a time of love, a time of peace, a time to remember Christ. . . ."

Myrna knew she was asleep. She had dreamed several times in the last week about Christmas back home. But the voices sounded so real. She opened her eyes. Perhaps she wasn't dreaming. Perhaps she had died and gone to heaven. For there were two angels in the doorway, two small angels in long white robes and tinsel halos. "Listen to the Christmas story." She lifted her glasses to her nose. They were there, all right. And then the angels came running at her.

"Merry Christmas, Grandma! Hi, Grandma!" And then the room was filled with them — not angels, but people; live, real people, surging toward her, bending over her, kneeling around her, embracing her, kissing her. "Merry Christmas, Mother!" "Surprise, Grandma!" "Are you surprised, Grandma?" "Merry Christmas!" "Merry Christmas!"

Myrna looked from face to face, openmouthed and silent. She was not dreaming. She was not dead. They were here, all of them. Her family was here — for Christmas.

One of them laughed and spoke. Was it Joy? "The kids made us promise to surprise you, Mother. You know how they love surprises. We've been planning it for months."

"Were you surprised, Grandma? Were you?"

Myrna nodded and tried to find

her voice. "I — I —"

Patricia squealed. "She was surprised!"

"Guess what, Grandma?" Was that Bradley, that tall boy with the broad smile? "We rented this huge house right by the beach — you can see the ocean from the window. We're all going to go there for Christmas. We rented it for a whole week!"

Myrna looked over at Joy, as if to ask if what she had heard was true.

Joy laughed again. "That's right, Mother. We rented a house on the beach. We decided we'd all take our vacations now instead of during the summer. I mean, who wants Christmas in Idaho when you can have a little sunshine, huh?"

"And the beach!"

"And Disneyland!"

"And Grandma!"

"Especially Grandma!"

That was Dale. At least Myrna thought it was Dale. She was having a hard time seeing. Something kept blurring her vision and she had to wipe her eyes.

Finally Myrna's voice worked. "You're — here? You're *all* here?" She looked around the room. There must have been thirty people crowded into that little room. Besides Florence, who was watching in amazement as if she was seeing a surprising scene in a movie.

"Yep. All of us." That was Susie. "We drove all night."

"Well, not quite all of us." That

was Beverly. "Not yet."

Myrna looked around, mentally calling the roll. "Richard. Where's Richard?"

"Richard will be here tomorrow," Beverly went on. "He's flying in tomorrow afternoon. With Genevieve."

Myrna looked at Beverly strangely. Maybe this was a dream. "What?"

"With *Genevieve*. Your friend from the rest home in Idaho Falls."

Myrna slowly turned to look at Florence, who was slowly turning to look at her.

"Genevieve?" asked Myrna again.

"Genevieve is coming here?" asked Florence.

"For Christmas!" continued Beverly. "Well, you don't think we would just let her sit there all alone in the rest home on Christmas, do you?"

The two women continued to stare at each other. Then Florence said softly, "Genevieve is coming *here?*"

"For *Christmas?*" added Myrna.

"Well, I'll admit we're having a little trouble locating her, Mother. We couldn't find a Rosemont Convalescent in Idaho Falls, but there was a *Rosewood* not too far away, so we figured that's what you meant. Only they didn't have a Genevieve Christensen. But they did have a Geneva Christopherson, which we decided had to be her. However, she had been transferred to a rest home in Boise last week, but we couldn't find out which one. So we sent Richard to Boise to find her. We got two plane tickets for tomorrow, the twenty-fourth. We weren't sure whether she needed a wheelchair, so we told the airline to have one ready just in case. We told Richard just not to bother to get on the plane unless he's got Genevieve with him. So don't worry, Mother. He'll find her."

"And you two get the best room, Grandma. It looks right out onto the ocean!"

"See what we made in the car coming down?" One of the twins held up two large, red felt stockings, with names sewn across the tops in white sequins — "Myrna" and "Genevieve."

"Do you think she'll like it?"

"Why . . . why, I think . . ." Myrna attempted to reply.

Dale knelt down and took her hand. "Are you all right, Mother? Is something wrong?"

Tears were streaming down Myrna's face as she reached over and put a hand on her son's cheek. "You bought . . . a plane ticket for Genevieve?"

Dale nodded. "She'll be here tomorrow."

With difficulty, Myrna continued speaking. "Dale —" She looked around the room, looked at the thirty or so faces that were watching her in anticipation. "There is no Genevieve."

Dale leaned in a little. "Pardon me?"

"There is no Genevieve. We made her up. Florence and I — we made her up."

Beverly knelt down and took her mother's other hand. "You made her up? *Why?*"

"Well, Florence didn't think that anybody would take in a little old lady for Christmas, and I said that yes, they would. And she said 'Who?' and I said, 'My children.' And she said no they wouldn't and I said they would. And it got to be terribly important, and so I had to find out. I . . . I had to find out . . . if I *taught* you anything."

There was a long silence, broken by Joy's loud laugh.

137

"If you *taught* us anything! Well, for Pete's sake, Mother, you don't remember what you taught us?"

"Well, I guess I had to know — if you *learned.*"

"You mean . . ." Julie's voice was full of disappointment. "We can't have Genevieve for Christmas?"

Sadly Myrna shook her head.

All were silent for a moment. And then Beverly stood up and walked over to the wheelchair and knelt down beside it. "Uh — Florence." Then she looked back at Myrna. "This *is* Florence, I presume?"

Myrna nodded.

"You started this whole thing, did you, Florence?"

Florence nodded and looked at the floor.

"Well. What are you doing for Christmas, Florence? Are you going anywhere?"

Florence's eyes traveled up to Beverly's face and she shook her head.

"How about coming with us? We seem to have an extra place here, now that Genevieve can't make it."

Florence surveyed the thirty or so faces that were looking at her and smiling. "Me? Go with you?"

"That's right."

"For — Christmas?"

"For a whole week — if you can stand us."

"Hey, yeah!" said the twin with the red stockings. "I can make another stocking!"

And the other twin cried out, "I speak first to push her wheel-chair on the beach!"

"Me next!"

Then all of them were laughing. Except for those who were crying. And then some were laughing and crying at the same time. Myrna was doing both. And so was Florence.

"You're sure — you're sure you've got room?" asked Florence hopefully.

"There's always room for one more!"

Myrna looked around to see who had said that, said it just the same way she had always said it. But she couldn't see. And it didn't matter anyway.

One more person squeezed her way into the crowded room. Ruth headed for the closet and pulled out a small suitcase. "I heard all that. I got Myrna packed while she was asleep. Now I'll really have to hustle to get Florence ready."

"Ruth?" asked Myrna weakly. "Aren't you off today?"

"Well, do you think I'd miss this?" Ruth gestured to the crowd and then began to load the suitcase with things from the closet and the chest of drawers. "They let me in on this, and I've been looking forward to it since Thanksgiving."

Beverly clapped her hands for attention. "Okay, let's get moving. Everybody out but Dale and me.

We'll see you soon at the house. Susie, remember to stop for the candles for the gingerbread house."

"Gingerbread house?" Florence reached out and touched Beverly's arm. "We're having a gingerbread house?"

"We'll have to make it tonight. We were afraid it might get broken in the car."

"Ruth?" Florence's tone was regal again and her spine was straighter than it had been for days. "Be sure to pack my red dress — the one with the lace."

"You bet, Florence. You bet."

The room was empty now except for the two women and Ruth and Beverly and Dale. Dale sat down at the small table and reached for the telephone. He dialed, and then paused for a moment. "Operator? I need the numbers of all the rest homes in Boise. Yes, I'll wait."

As they made their way down the hall, Florence in her wheelchair and Myrna with her cane, they smiled and wished a Merry Christmas to everyone they met. And the smell of Turkey Surprise came from the kitchen. And the tree in the lobby, donated and decorated by the grade-school children down the street, looked bright and beautiful. And the strains of "Silent Night" came softly through the intercom. "Glory streams from thy holy face, with the dawn of redeeming grace. . . ." And a voice, a long-ago-and-far-away voice that was closer than any voice can ever get, spoke with a soft satisfaction: *"Ye took me in. I was a stranger, and ye took me in."*

The doors opened and they moved on out into the December sunlight.